?? WHY DO WE DO THAT ??

DJ Selvidge

Copyright © 2015 DJ Selvidge

All rights reserved.

ISBN: 1494926571
ISBN-13: 978-1494926571

DEDICATION

This book is dedicated to my best friend and husband, Wayne Selvidge, who never fails to encourage me to follow my dreams and believes I can accomplish whatever I set out to do.

CONTENTS

	Acknowledgments	i
1	Anglo Saxons and Other Ancient Pagans	1
2	Christmas Traditions	17
3	Other Holiday Traditions	27
4	Miscellaneous Traditions	64

ACKNOWLEDGMENTS

I would like to offer my thanks to my friend Sherri Anderson for her encouragement and willingness to review my drafts, my friend Jan Peterson for helping me to remember the traditions I had overlooked, and my family for their unbelievable patience throughout the writing process.

A special remembrance is due to my late friend, Dave Kocsis, who gave me the gift of providing an author photo for my books. May he rest in peace.

1 ANGLO SAXONS AND OTHER ANCIENT PAGANS

Every Little Girl's Dream

Wherever weddings are celebrated around the world, you can be certain they will be steeped in tradition. Our own customs here in the United States were brought over from Europe and passed down to us through the years. While their origins have long been forgotten, they continue to be important rituals at wedding after wedding.

I think most people would be amused if they knew the origins of the traditions we practice so religiously today. For example, did you know the reason most weddings are performed in the spring? Well, way back when, spring was associated with fertility and new life but, even more importantly, it was when the weather was warmer and people bathed.

In olden times, before Europe was quite so civilized, the Anglo Saxon people lived in small villages where there may not be an available young woman. If a young man wanted a bride he would have to steal one from another village. He would enlist the help of his "best man" (strongest friend) to help him and they would kidnap a young lady, carrying her off against her will to the wedding. Young women brought along to assist with the bride were called bridesmaids.

At the ceremony, the bride always stood to the groom's left. This would enable him to hold her there while leaving his right, or dominant hand, free for his sword should someone show up to rescue the bride. The best man was also responsible to help defend against rescuers (or competitors). The celebration festivities began with the groom's first dance which consisted of parading his stolen bride around to show off his hunting skills.

Afterwards, the bride was carried off to honeymoon in a secluded place where rescuers would be unable to find her. Since brides often did not go willingly, they had to be carried across the threshold. Usually, by the time the bride's family located her, fear that she could already be pregnant caused unwilling parents to go ahead and negotiate the bride price.

As European customs became more civilized, arranged marriages came into being. A man's daughters would be strategically married to secure needed family alliances. The Anglo Saxon word 'wedd' actually means 'gamble or wager' and thus the bride price was paid, the alliance was secured, and the gentleman took his chances on his bride.

Agreements back then were sealed with a kiss, which was legally binding, and so the wedding kiss was introduced. The bride wore a veil to the altar and the groom was not allowed to see her before the ceremony to prevent the groom from being disappointed and backing out. Since the groom was not to see in, the bride could not see out and the father of the bride had to escort his daughter down the aisle to the waiting groom. It was not until after the ceremony was completed and it was time for the ceremonial kiss that the veil was lifted and the groom was able to see his bride for the first time.

In the 14th century, a piece of the bride's dress was considered good luck and many a bride was injured when guests literally tore her dress to pieces trying to come away with a good remnant. Thus, brides began protecting themselves by throwing things, usually pieces of undergarments, to the guests. Occasionally, the men would become drunk and try to remove the garter ahead of time so it became practice for the groom to remove the garter personally and toss it to the men. Brides then began tossing their bouquets to the ladies.

When an Anglo Saxon threw his shoe, it indicated that authority had been transferred. For that reason, the custom was that the groom would strike the bride with her own shoe, symbolizing his authority over her. Willing brides would then throw the shoes at their bridesmaids to see who would marry next. Later, in Tudor England, guests would throw shoes at the Bride & Groom believing it was good luck if they hit the couple or their carriage, a custom believed to be a throwback to the angry father throwing shoes at the kidnapping groom. Today we still tie shoes on the back of the couple's car for good luck.

Few people know that the first wedding cakes were

actually wheat bread which was thrown at the head of the bride or broken over her head. Nor do many people realize that the original plain white wedding robes were meant to symbolize poverty showing that the bride brought nothing to the marriage and the groom was, therefore, not responsible for her debts.

While it is safe to say that many of our traditions did not begin as things a bride necessarily would have chosen, they have endured through the years and are still widely practiced. And since their origins have often been forgotten, these traditions are remembered fondly today and have somehow become the essence of little girls' hopes and dreams.

Masks and Beads and Revelry

To many Americans, the term "Mardi Gras" brings to mind a season of revelry in New Orleans where drunken tourists throw beads off balconies to women baring their breasts in the French Quarter of the city. Nothing could be further from the truth. It may surprise some to learn that Mardi Gras is, in fact, a religious holiday, steeped in tradition, with its origins dating back not to France, as many believe, but even earlier to ancient Rome. It seems the annual pagan observance of Lupercalia, celebrating Spring and fertility, was very much like our modern day indulgences of the pleasures of life and came at this same changeover time of year. When Christianity came to Rome, the religious leaders thought it would be more prudent to incorporate the local tradition into Christianity than to try and eliminate it. People were encouraged to binge or feast on meat, cheese, eggs, and fat in order to empty their homes of them prior to Lent when they would eat only fish or fast. The practice eventually spread to other European countries.

In Medieval times, this day before Lent was used by feudal Lords and gentry to ride through the countryside bestowing cakes, coins, and trinkets on the local peasants. This may be the origins of the modern practice of Kings' cakes and throwing coins and trinkets at Mardi Gras. Also, parties and balls were thrown in recognition of those being welcomed into Knighthood. The term "Mardi Gras" means "Fat Tuesday" in French and may come from the practice in old times of parading a fat ox through the streets of Paris on this day or from the practice of using up all the fats in the house since they were strictly forbidden during Lent.

Mardi Gras came to the United States when the French explorers Iberville and Bienville landed just south of what is today New Orleans on March 3, 1699. They held a small celebration of the day and then named the spot Point du Mardi Gras. Bienville also named the nearby tributary Bayou Mardi Gras. In the years following, New Orleans and other French settlements in the area continued having street celebrations, masked balls, and huge feasts in honor of the day.

When the Spanish took control of New Orleans, they abolished the Mardi Gras celebrations and no more were held until Louisiana became a state in 1812. Then, in 1827, a group of college students, attempting to copy what they had seen done in Paris, danced through the streets of the city wearing colorful costumes. And ten years later, the first Mardi Gras parade was held in New Orleans.

In 1857, a group of businessmen organized the very first secret society for the purpose of conducting a torchlit Mardi Gras procession. They were called the Mistick Krewe of Comus. Since that time, many other krewes have been established and conduct multiple parades during the Mardi Gras season in New Orleans. The Krewes ride on the floats and throw coins and trinkets to the crowds. Keep in mind, one cannot just join a Krewe... one must be invited.

Carnival is another word for Mardi Gras. It comes from the word carnelevarium meaning 'to remove meat'. At one time, these celebrations lasted 3 days, during the Shrovetide (Sunday, Monday, Shrove Tuesday). Now, the festivities begin around Epiphany, or Kings' Day (January 6th), which is the 12th Day of Christmas, and run through Fat Tuesday, thus filling the gap between Christmas and Easter.

The colors of Mardi Gras were established in 1872 by King Rex, the King of Carnival. Purple represents justice, green represents faith, and gold represents power. Similarly, the masks represent the dead who want to return to their homes at this celebratory time of year. King Rex is still very much part of Mardi Gras today and it is the Krewes' responsibility to re-elect him "King of the Carnival" each year.

Of course, what would Mardi Gras be without the traditional eating of pancakes? In the churches of England, pancake suppers were a common occurrence. On this day, pancake feasts were held to try and use up the milk, eggs, and fat which could not be eaten during Lent. The women's pancake bell run is also common on this day in England and, as the story goes, it all started back in Olney in 1445. One woman making pancakes heard the church bell ring calling folks to confession on Shrove Tuesday. In her hurry to get to the church, she ran the whole way with her frying pan in hand, flipping the pancakes as she went. An annual race to the church developed for women over 18, who must be wearing an apron and bonnet, and flipping pancakes along the course. This race continued every year until, in 1850, the women in Liberal, KS, issued a challenge to the women of Olney. The race was run in two countries with race times being compared by transatlantic telephone as it is still run today in the two locations. The prize? A kiss of peace from the bell ringer, a prayer book from the local vicar, and a frying pan.

And finally, what is not a Mardi Gras tradition? The practice many people think of where young tourist women bare their breasts in order to have beads thrown to them from the balconies of New Orleans' hotels is not only NOT a Mardi Gras tradition, it is actually illegal in New Orleans and can result in arrest. This activity really only occurs in the French Quarter, and mostly on Bourbon Street. In fact, none of the Mardi Gras parades in New Orleans even come down Bourbon Street though the news media have made this street in the French Quarter famous for its post parade debauchery. The true Mardi Gras celebrations in the city are free entertainment and usually quite family friendly.

?? WHY DO WE DO THAT ??

The Bunny and the Egg

A long time ago there lived a group of people called the Ancient Anglo Saxons. Each year in the spring, the Anglo Saxons would hold a carnival which they called Eostre (named after the Teutonic goddess of dawn, spring and fertility). These rites of spring were always celebrated in her honor at the vernal equinox (first day of spring) each year. This pagan festival included rabbits, which were the most fertile animals known at the time, and colored eggs as symbols of fertility and rebirth. As this pagan culture converted to Christianity, they continued the celebration in honor of Christ's Resurrection since the religious commemoration fell at about the same time of year and also emphasized rebirth (through faith in Jesus Christ). The colored eggs and bunnies eventually came to be known as Easter Eggs and Easter Bunnies.

In medieval times, egg throwing became a church tradition. The priest would throw a hard-boiled egg to one of the boys in the choir. This boy would toss it to the next who would toss it again and whoever held the egg when the clock struck 12 was the winner. The prize, of course, was the manhandled egg.

The Easter bunny was brought to the United States by the Pennsylvania Dutch (German settlers in Pennsylvania in the 1700s). The German children tried to be very good so the Easter Bunny would lay a nest of colored eggs for them. They would use their caps and bonnets to build nests in the house, yard or barn. Eventually, American kids picked up on the tradition and replaced the caps and bonnets with fancy baskets which were made to look like nests. And even though the Easter bunny could lay eggs, he was typically thought to be a male rabbit named Peter.

In the 1800's, the first edible bunnies appeared in Germany made of pastry and sugar. Later, in the United States, these became chocolate bunnies unlike in England, where it's the Easter eggs that are chocolate.

At one time, Eggs were used by the Romans who gave them out as prizes in their Easter races. Eventually, this led to the introduction of the Easter Egg Roll. The egg roll was intended to represent Christ's rolling away the stone from the tomb and the rules were simple. Whoever could roll their egg the farthest down a hill without breaking it was the winner. Easter egg hunts eventually evolved from this practice of rolling decorated eggs. In the United States, the Easter egg hunt has become institutionalized with large Easter egg hunts held every year on the White House lawn.

And, to this day, the egg and the bunny continue to live together happily ever after.

When is Easter?

Ever confused over what day Easter falls on? Up until 325 AD, Easter was celebrated on different days of the week, but in that year, Emperor Constantine's Council of Nicaea issued the Easter Rule. This rule stated that Easter would be celebrated on the first Sunday after the first full moon on or after the vernal equinox. The vernal equinox is always March 21st so Easter is celebrated the first Sunday after the first full moon on or after March 21st. Huh?!?

Trick or Treat

About 2000 years ago in the area now known as Ireland, the United Kingdom, and Northern France, there lived an ancient Celtic people. Before the Romans arrived in 43 A.D., the Celts were a pagan people who believed that their priests, known as Druids, had the ability to commune with the dead. This ability was believed to be much more powerful on Samhain, (pronounced Sow-in), the last day of the Celtic year. On this night, which fell on October 31st, the veil between the living and the dead would be at its thinnest and the spirits of those who had died during the year traveled into the other world. It was also believed that the Druids could make easier predictions for the future with the unliving around.

The Celts believed that on Samhain, ghosts and other ghoulish creatures would return to the world of the living, causing trouble and damaging crops, walking among the living. However, this was a time when they also felt especially close to their deceased friends and relatives. On this day, they would set places for them at the table, light candles to help them along on their journeys back to the spirit world, and set out food and wine as treats for them. The Celts would wear costumes of animal skins to avoid being recognized by ghosts on this night and masks to be mistaken for fellow spirits.

The main focus of the Samhain celebration were the

community bonfires which were lit to honor the dead, aid them in their journeys, and to keep them away from the living. Families would extinguish the fires in their homes before venturing out to join in the bonfire activities of singing, dancing, and storytelling. Animal and fruit sacrifices were made to the Celtic deities to help keep the unliving at bay. When the morning light came, each would take home some of the fire to relight the fires in their homes. This was believed to bring good fortune for the coming year.

With the arrival of the Romans, the celebration evolved as it was combined with Feralia, a time in late October when the Romans commemorated the dead. The celebration also became intertwined with the Roman Day of Pomona, a harvest celebration of the goddess of fruit and trees whose symbol is an apple. The game of bobbing for apples is believed to have originated from these early celebrations.

Following the arrival of the Romans, of course, came the arrival of the Catholic Church. In 601 A.D., Pope Gregory the First had decided that, rather than wipe out pagan holidays, they should be transformed into something which was God-honoring. So... somewhere around the 8th century, the wandering spirits, believed by the Celts to be mischievous, were deemed by the Catholic Church to be evil. In an attempt to draw people's attention to a more Godly focus, Pope Gregory III established November 1st as All Saints' Day in honor of all Saints and Martyrs.

This day was also called All Hallows, and the day before, All Hallows Eve, which is where we get the word Halloween.

But the church did not realize how strong a connection existed to the old beliefs. As the new Christians began to focus on Saints and Martyrs, they did not give up their fascination with the dead. Eventually, still trying to transform the pagan practices, the church instituted a new observance on November 2nd called All Souls' Day to pay homage to the dead, or souls who had passed and to offer prayers intended to comfort their souls and elevate them from Purgatory. Dressing in animal costumes was replaced with dressing as saints, angels, and devils. The day was celebrated with big bonfires and parades, but to replace leaving food and wine for wandering spirits, the church instituted a practice called 'souling'. Poor people could beg at the doors of houses for pastries called 'soul cakes' in exchange for a promise to pray for the family's dead relatives.

As time went on, people began dressing like more and more dreadful creatures and performing for food and other treats. Eventually the practice involved begging for sweets. Called 'mumming', this is believed to be the beginning of trick-or-treating and was brought to the United States by Irish immigrants.

2 CHRISTMAS TRADITIONS

The Evolution of St. Nicholas

St. Nicholas was born in the third century in Turkey, in a village then known as Patara, Lycia to a wealthy family. Nicholas dedicated his life to serving God and was made Bishop of Myra while still a young man. Bishop Nicholas became known throughout the land for his generosity to those in need, his love for children, and his concern for sailors and ships.

It is said that Nicholas once learned of a poor man who had three daughters. Because their father could not afford a dowry for them, the daughters had no hope of marriage and would be sold into slavery. This would sentence them to a certain life of prostitution. On three separate evenings, Bishop Nicholas threw a bag of gold through an upstairs window providing a dowry for each of the daughters, thus saving them from being sold. As the story goes, the bags of gold landed in stockings hanging by the fire to dry and in shoes placed on the hearth.

St. Nicholas Day is celebrated each year on the anniversary of his death - Dec 6, 343. Dressed in his red bishop's robes, he is said to bring gifts to children just as he did in many of the stories told about him through the ages. And, in memory of the three daughters he saved from being sold into slavery, he comes early while the children are still sleeping and leaves presents. Before children go to sleep they place a bowl or plate under their bed, hang a stocking by the fireplace or put a pair of shoes in front of the door (varies by country). In Europe, this early advent gift-giving on St. Nicholas Day helps to preserve a Christmas Day focus on the Christ Child.

In Germany, Martin Luther replaced the name of the gift bringer with the Christ Child, or, in German, Christkindl. Through the years, this was eventually mispronounced enough that it became Kriss Kringle, another name by which we know St. Nicholas. But, brought to the United States by immigrants, the English speaking children often mispronounced the Dutch version of his name, Sinterklaas, and he eventually became known to us here in the U.S. as Santa Claus.

Now, in order to convince folks that Coke was not just a summer drink, the Coca-Cola Company began featuring Santa on their bottles to depict the idea that the beverage could be consumed at any time of the year. Until that time, Santa had traditionally worn Nicholas' red bishop's robe, as we see on early Santa figures; he changed from Bishop's attire to a red suit with trousers in the United States when he began appearing on the Coke bottles.

Today, St. Nicholas continues to evolve each year as songs, television specials, and movies spin new and ever changing details about Santa, reindeer, and the North Pole. Changing at a pace never before seen, it is my belief that our children's children will know a completely different St. Nick than we do today as he is already hardly recognizable as the Bishop of Myra.

The Story of the Advent Wreath

I have never really liked the term "Black Friday". Not being a fan of shopping, the idea of going near a store on this, the retail extravaganza of the year, is incredibly horrifying to me. To follow a day of giving thanks to our Heavenly Father for all His good gifts by such an extreme commercial act just seems the wrong way to start the Christmas season somehow. We have made it our tradition, instead, to drag out the Christmas decorations, tree, etc. and transform our home. It is the official start of the Christmas season at our house.

That is what the word advent means... the beginning, commencement, onset. It is a season of waiting. For Christians, we celebrate not only the ancient coming of the Messiah to be born in Bethlehem, but we also anticipate and prepare for His ultimate return at the Second Coming. The advent season begins with the fourth Sunday before Christmas, which coincidentally just happens to be the Sunday closest to my birthday (November 30th). Thus, it is always easy for me to remember.

Advent is a season of expectation and anticipation. It should be a time of preparation and hope for the Messiah who will bring peace and righteousness into the world. The advent ring (wreath) is designed to reflect the Christmas story and the promise it holds to all people.

The wreath is a circle which reminds us of God Himself. He is eternal, without beginning or end. The life and salvation He offers is also eternal which is symbolized in the evergreens woven into the wreath. As the winter comes and the leaves die on the other trees, the life remains visible in the evergreens throughout the long, cold months. Candles symbolize light. Jesus brings light into a world of darkness and sin. And when we accept Jesus as our Savior, we are called to become the light of the world. As more people become Christians, the light shines brighter and brighter and spreads.

The four candles in the circle are for the four Sundays before Christmas. Three are purple and one is pink. Purple is, of course, the color of royalty, as Christ is the King of Kings and Lord of Lords. The pink candle is used on the third of the four Sundays, and is the joy candle. In some circles it is called Gaudete Sunday, from the Latin word for "rejoice". The pink represents a change of emphasis, for one week, from the repentance before the Lord, to celebration and rejoicing at the coming of the King and the salvation that He will bring. The fourth week marks a return to the preparation phase and a purple candle acknowledging His royalty and Kingship. The four candles, or weeks, represent a time of waiting, and represent as follows:

Prophets - Hope
Bethlehem - Love
Shepherds - Joy
Angels - Peace.

The first candle is lit the first Sunday. An additional candle is lit each succeeding Sunday until all four are lit on the final Sunday before Christmas representing how the light and love of Christ spread gradually throughout the world. A large, white candle stands in the center of the wreath. It is white for purity and righteousness. It is the Christ candle and is lit on Christmas Eve or Christmas Day. It reminds us that Christ is the center of our celebration and brings light into the world. For many, the candles will burn through Epiphany (January 6th) or the twelfth day of Christmas.

As we enter each advent season, it will be my sincere desire to put aside busyness and the commercial trappings of the Christmas retailers and examine my heart in preparation for the Coming King. Who will join me in the pursuit of a pure heart as we seek to find the hope, love, joy, and peace that only Christ the King can bring?

The Twelve Days of Christmas

Many people believe that the Twelve Days of Christmas occur during the days leading up to Christmas. Actually, that is not correct. The Twelve Days begin on Christmas Day (December 25th) and run through Epiphany (January 6th). This period of time is also known to many of us as Christmastide, Yuletide, or Twelvetide. But don't be confused... the twelve nights run from Christmas Eve (December 24th through January 5th.

Initially, gifts were distributed to their recipients during the course of the twelve days, as is seen in Drennon's famous song, "The Twelve Days of Christmas". Today, however, these twelve days and nights are celebrated differently in different places around the world. In some countries, gifts are only given on Christmas Day while in other places they are given only on the Twelfth Night or, in some places, on each of the twelve nights.

But how did all of this get started? Many believe that the lengthy holiday season is patterned after the Germanic Yuletide or possibly even the Roman Saturnalia, pagan customs though they may be. We know that during the Middle Ages, these twelve days in England consisted of continuous feasting and 'merrymaking'. Today, countries in the United Kingdom and the Commonwealth still celebrate many of the Christmastide traditions such as Boxing

Day, plum pudding, and Wassail.

When the early colonists came to the new world from England, they adapted their own version of the twelve days for their new country. This version acquired variations through the years becoming uniquely American. It is believed the Christmas wreath originated with the colonists who made these decorations for their doors out of the local pine. It was tradition to make these on Christmas Eve and then to hang them on the door through either the Twelfth Night or Epiphany morning.

The Twelfth Day, Epiphany, is the day set aside to remember the visit of the Magi (wise men), or kings from the east. In many countries, a king's cake, is baked for Epiphany. The cake is baked with a real fava bean inside. Whoever finds the fève is obligated to provide the cake next year. His partner, likewise, is obligated to provide next year's champagne. In some English-speaking countries, it is believed to be unlucky to leave Christmas decorations up past the Twelfth Night or Epiphany morning, though in non-English speaking countries, they are often left up until Candlemas (February 2nd).

The Nutcracker

The original German nutcrackers (Nussknackers) were developed in the mountainous Erzgebirge region of Germany. The main source of employment for many of the villagers in these Mountains was in the mines, but during the harsh winter months, it was not possible to go to the mines to work. An alternative source of income was needed and wood carving became the main source of income for poor families. Life was hard for these miners who worked long hours and were often taken advantage of by their superiors. Since Germans sometimes say someone has "a hard nut to crack" if they mean that the person is having difficulties, these 18th century woodworkers who created the now traditional form of nutcracker made the nutcracker figures in the shape of the people who made their life difficult. Thus, the nutcrackers were made to resemble kings, soldiers, and other authority figures. While in life the lower classes were at the mercy of sometimes harsh authorities, in their homes the tables could be turned by making figures of those authorities perform work for the poorer people.

3 OTHER HOLIDAY TRADITIONS

Auld Lang Syne

We've all sung "Auld Lang Syne" at New Year's Eve to ring in the new year. The song is derived from a Scottish poem written by Robert Burns in 1788. But by Burns' own admission, the poem is not totally his. He gave credit to having been told the poem by an old man when he sent the poem to The Scots Musical Museum. The song itself bears striking resemblance to another poem printed years earlier in 1711 by a poet named James Watson called "Old Long Syne". Auld Lang Syne means "old long since" or "for the sake of old times". In British countries, it is sung on other occasions as well as New Year's Eve, but having been brought to the United States, its use at New Year's Eve has been the tradition that has prevailed.

It is the original Scottish custom that when the song is sung, everyone joins hands to form a circle around the dance floor. When the last verse begins, everyone crosses their arms over their chest so that their right arm is extended to the person on their left. When the song finishes, everyone rushes to the center of the circle, turns under their arms (still holding hands), and finishes facing outward.

Black-Eyed Peas

If you're planning to celebrate New Year's Eve in the South, chances are you're planning on eating black-eyed peas. These healthy legumes are a tradition which symbolize prosperity in the New Year because they swell when they cook. They are eaten with greens (collard, turnip, or mustard), which represent money, some form of pork, which represents positive motion (because pigs root forward), and cornbread, which represents gold.

Eating black-eyed peas is a Jewish good luck tradition. Black-eyed peas are one of the good luck symbols eaten on Rosh Hashanah, the Jewish New Year. This practice has been followed by Sephardi and Israeli Jews for a long time and was brought to the United States when the first Sephardi Jews arrived in Georgia in the 1730's. These Jews are still there to this day. However, the practice of eating the black-eyed peas was not adopted by non-Jews until the Civil War.

During Sherman's March to the Sea (The Savannah Campaign) in 1864, William T. Sherman directed his troops to take everything they found of value (food, crops, livestock), and destroy what they couldn't carry. As his troops marched through the South from Atlanta to Savannah, they left little of value for the Southerners.

Now it seems, in the North, black-eyed peas were only used for feeding livestock. They were never eaten by people. And since Sherman's men had taken all the livestock, they saw no reason to destroy the large stores of field peas which they could not carry away. The destitute Southerners, left with virtually nothing, considered this oversight to be their own good luck and were literally saved from starvation by eating the black-eyed peas.

Many variations to this tradition have developed through the years. Some folks add a shiny new penny or dime to the pot. Whoever gets the coin in their bowl can expect extra good luck during the year. Some people believe that the peas should be the first food eaten in the New Year, eating them shortly after midnight. And some folks say you must eat exactly 365 peas for the best chance of good luck.

?? WHY DO WE DO THAT ??

Is It Spring Yet?

We've all heard of Punxsutawny Phil, that infamous little groundhog who shows his head bright and early on a February morning in Punxsutawny, Pennsylvania each year to predict the early arrival of Spring. And, as many know, he has a good friend named Wiarton Willy, who is responsible for predicting the weather in Canada. Such an enormous job for two such small fellows. How did they get such a big responsibility?

Groundhog Day is celebrated on February 2nd, or Candlemas, which falls halfway between the Winter Solstice and the Spring Equinox. Candlemas is the day set aside to remember the day of the Christ Child's presentation at the Temple on the day of Mary's Purification after His birth. European superstition once held that if it was sunny on Candlemas, an additional six weeks of winter weather would occur. If it was cloudy, Spring would come early. The Germans used an animal (usually a badger or a hedgehog) as an instrument to determine whether or not it was sunny out on this day. When the German settlers came to Pennsylvania, they brought this practice with them and adopted the groundhog as their animal indicator. The first "official" trip to Gobbler's Knob in Punxsutawny on Groundhog Day to obtain Phil's prediction was made in 1887 by a group of groundhog hunters known as "The Punxsutawney Groundhog Club." Today, the largest Groundhog Day celebration is still conducted in Punxsutawny though celebrations are held in a number of other states and various Amish communities.

Wherefore art thou, Valentine?

Valentine's Day is usually believed to have originated as a day of commemoration for Saint Valentine, a Roman who was martyred for his faith on February 14, 269 A.D. As it happened, St. Valentine's Day fell on Lupercalia, the Roman festival of wolves. On this day, men and women would choose partners for the day and celebrate fertility. The men would playfully whip the women and then couples would pair up for fertility rites. In more modern times, Italian couples sit and read poetry together, or listen to music though, in Rome, St Valentine's Day is still known as Lupercalia, a very romantic and pleasure-loving occasion.

Over time, February 14th became associated with love, romance and sweethearts. St. Valentine's Day has spread around the globe and is even popular in many countries where the government has specifically banned it. No matter where you are or how you celebrate, one thing seems evident...love is truly universal.

In Europe, during the Middle Ages, single people would draw names from a bowl to determine whom their valentines would be and then wear these names on their sleeves for one week. This is where we get the expression "wearing your heart on your sleeve" to mean that it is easy for other people to know your feelings.

In olden times, women used to watch for birds flying overhead on St. Valentine's Day. It was believed to be an indication of whom the woman would marry:

>   robin - she would marry a sailor.
> sparrow - she would marry a poor man but be very happy
> goldfinch - she would marry a millionaire

In Denmark, a transparency is sent which is known as a lover's card. When held up to the light, you can see a picture of a lover handing his love a gift. People also trade poems and candy snowdrops. Joking letters, gaekkebrev, are sent with the sender's name signed as dots. If the recipient can guess the correct person, they will send that person a candy egg at Easter.

In France, there used to be a tradition known as Calling for Valentines. This custom involved unmarried men and women going into houses which faced each other and then calling out across from one window to the other, hoping to pair off with the one they have chosen. If the young man didn't care for the valentine he was paired with, he would desert her. Afterwards, a bonfire was lit where the young ladies who had been deserted would yell out abuse while burning images of the deserters. Eventually, the French government came out against this practice as it culminated in not-so-loving incidents.

?? WHY DO WE DO THAT ??

In Scotland, St. Valentine's Day is celebrated as a festival during which an equal amount of single men and women get together. Each writes their name (sometimes their real name...sometimes not) on a piece of paper which is then rolled up. The names are placed in two hats and a drawing is held, splitting the group into couples. Gifts are given to the ladies who then wear the name of their valentines over their hearts or on their sleeves. There is often a dance and sometimes even romances or marriage after the festival. It is common practice for established lovers to give each other a love token or a true love knot.

Germans love flowers which is evident on St. Valentine's Day. Large bouquets of flowers are chosen for that special lady but they must be her favorites. This shows that the man has been paying attention and doesn't just think of her as "any girl".

In Victorian England, elaborate Valentine's Day cards used to be given among family and friends. This custom was then taken to Australia where elaborate valentines were made out of a satin cushion. The cushion was perfumed and decorated with flowers and shells. A taxidermed humming bird or bird of paradise was also included and then the valentine would be delivered in a decorated box.

In Korea and Japan, young women give candies to their boyfriends. While the Korean women buy these chocolates, the Japanese women think it is not true love unless they make the chocolates themselves.

There is another special day called 'White Day" on March 14 which is just the opposite of St. Valentine's Day. Young men give chocolates to their girlfriends and confess their love. Young people in Korea who have no girlfriend or boyfriend have another special day called 'Black Day' on April 14. On this day, they eat Jajang noodles with friends who are similarly unattached.

In Taiwan, St. Valentine's Day is celebrated February 14th, but there is also a special Valentine's Day on the Seventh Day of the Seventh Month of the Chinese lunar calendar. This second day is based on a Chinese fairy tale from long ago. Both are important days to send flowers. These flowers can contain a host of messages. One red rose means an only love while eleven roses mean a favorite. Ninety-nine roses mean forever but one hundred and eight are a marriage proposal.

Here in the United States, roses also symbolize both love and forgiveness. White roses are for true love, red roses are for passion, and yellow roses are for friendship. Black roses mean farewell.

Wearing of the Green

Many people don't realize this, but the original color associated with Saint Patrick was blue. So how did green become such a symbol of St. Patrick's Day and Ireland in general? Now some say it is because St Patrick, when he became a Christian, used the 3-leafed shamrock to explain the Holy Trinity to the Pagan Irish. But that is legend, and who is to say for sure whether it is true?

Still, the fact is, it has everything to do with the shamrock. This little plant was called the "seamroy" by the Celts and was considered a symbol of the return of spring each year. In the 17th century, the English ruled Ireland and the monarchy was attempting to achieve the suppression of the Gaelic way of life. Laws were passed against using the language of the land and forbidding the practice of Catholicism. Wearing a shamrock, or wearing of the green as it was called, began to be a symbol of Irish nationalism and pride in their heritage. It was a way of showing their opposition to English rule as the color green was used in the flags of several revolutionary groups in England. And shamrocks seemed to grow in abundance everywhere in Ireland.

Eventually, conditions in Ireland would lead to the 1798 Rebellion in which Irish soldiers wore green uniforms hoping to gain attention for their cause. Though defeated by the English, Irish Protestants and Catholics had been united in the cause and green became a lasting symbol for the Irish.

The term "Wearing of the Green" refers to the practice of wearing a shamrock on your clothing. Actually wearing green clothing is an Americanized version of this tradition and was never Irish at all. It is rumored that being pinched for not wearing green on St. Patrick's Day was thought up by American school children and I can find nothing anywhere to dispute this.

The green of St. Patrick's Day has spread even further and we see about everything from baked goods to beer died green these days. Our nation's White House dies its fountain green each year and the people of Chicago actually turn out to watch the city's river be died green.

Just a side note… While the three-leafed clover grows in abundance, the four-leafed clover is actually quite rare (they do occur) and thus it is considered to be very lucky if you find one.

Corned Beef and Cabbage

When it comes to lavish St. Patrick's Day celebrations, many people think of the Irish. But the truth is, St. Patrick's Day in Ireland used to be a Catholic feast day and relatively quiet. Now the Irish have observed this day for over 1000 years. Celebrated on the day believed to be St. Patrick's death, the usual observance was to attend church in the morning followed by feasting in the afternoon.

Because St. Patrick's Day occurs during the Lent season, Catholics would have been required to fast from eating meat or drinking leading up to the holiday. The church would allow its members to break this fast during the St. Patrick's Day celebrations, Lent prohibitions were waived, and people would dance, drink, and feast.

The traditional drink in Ireland at that time was beer and a traditional Irish dish was bacon and cabbage. This became the traditional meal served in Ireland for the celebrations. As the Irish immigrants came to the United States in the mid-1800s, money was tight and many could not afford bacon though cabbage was still largely eaten along with the Irish staple, potatoes. Soon, they learned about an affordable alternative to bacon from their Jewish neighbors, and corned beef replaced bacon in the Irish dish.

St. Patrick's Day celebrations were as quiet in the new world as they had been in Ireland at first. But Irish Americans, wanting to celebrate their ethnic heritage, began forming St. Patrick's Day parades in the larger cities. These started out as religious events primarily, but the holiday has lost its religious roots to a great extent as the Irish and non-Irish alike join in the fun. And now, the parades and the green beer and all the hoopla have found their way back to Ireland where the tourists are entertained by it all.

Mother's Day

The celebration of Mother's Day is a tradition that has spread to a multitude of countries. Many celebrate in much the same way as the United States with cards, flowers, and treating their moms to a special meal. And while the American way of celebrating has become the most usual, the origins of this holiday are varied.

Years ago, in Europe, early Christians celebrated the fourth Sunday in Lent in honor of the Virgin Mary. Several centuries ago, this holiday was extended to include all moms and was called 'Mothering Sunday'. At the time, children as young as eight or nine were often sent to work as apprentices or as servants in the homes of wealthy families. Though they were in nearby towns, transportation was hard to come by and they did not get to visit their families very often.

Before having to work through the Easter holiday, these servants would be given a weekend off during Lent when they were allowed to return home and visit their families. On the way there, they would pick wildflowers to give to their mothers or bring small gifts from those for whom they worked. This visit home during Lent was called 'going-a-mothering' and would end in the feast day known as 'Mothering Sunday', after which they would return to work and not see their families again until the

Christmas holiday.

As the European immigration came to the New World, the practice died out, though still celebrated in England. Mother's Day was reinvented in the United States, however, in 1870 by a woman named Julia Ward Howe. Though Howe had written the Battle Hymn of the Republic 12 years earlier, she was very discouraged and distraught by the destruction of the Civil War and called on all mothers to come together and protest the practice of mothers' sons killing other mothers' sons. Howe called for an International Day of Peace and Motherhood.

Howe's original proposal was to convert July 4th into a Mother's Day but, as it turned out, June 2nd was chosen in 1873. In that year, 18 cities celebrated the holiday… all funded by Howe. With time, as Howe stopped funding the celebrations, the celebrations stopped.

Mother's Day was resurrected in the United States by an Appalachian homemaker named Anna Jarvis. She organized a day to raise awareness of poor health conditions in her community calling it "Mothers Work Day". She believed that mothers would be the best ones to promote this. After her death in 1905, her daughter Anna sought to follow up on her belief that there were many days dedicated to men, but none to mothers. The younger Anna began to lobby among politicians and anyone who would listen in order to establish a day dedicated to mothers.

In 1908, Anna succeeding in arranging a church service in Grafton, WV to celebrate mothers and handed out white carnations to all mothers who attended. White carnations were her mother's favorite flower. Five years after that service, the House of Representatives adopted a resolution which called for federal government officials to wear white carnations on the second Sunday in May. The following year, President Woodrow Wilson signed a joint resolution making Mother's Day official.

In 1912, Anna obtained a trademark of the terms "2nd Sunday in May" and "Mother's Day". She also created the Mother's Day International Association. And even though she started the tradition of giving white carnations, in honor of her mother's favorite flower, in the 1920s Anna quit working to devote herself to fighting full-time the commercialism of the holiday brought about by the floral industry. She eventually died childless.

A Rose for Father

Though the celebration of Mother's Day was adopted quite quickly in the United States, this was not the case for its complement, Father's Day. Initially received with mockery and ridicule, Father's Day's path to acceptance was long and difficult. A male dominated Congress believed that the celebration would be perceived as self-applause and that the holiday would be exploited and commercialized by the vendors of male gifts. Advocates of the day had serious opposition to overcome.

The idea was first thought of in 1909 by a woman in Spokane, Washington by the name of Sonora Smart Dodd, while she was attending a Mother's Day sermon. Mrs. Dodd and her five brothers had been raised by her single parent father, William Jackson Smart, a Civil War veteran whose wife had died very young. Believing her father had contributed just as much to raising a successful family as any mother, and wanting to honor him, Mrs. Dodd proposed the first Father's Day and wanted to hold it on his birthday, June 5th. The local ministers and YMCA staff were very supportive but, not having time enough to prepare, postponed the day and the first celebration was held June 19, 1910 in the Spokane YMCA. People were urged to mark the day by wearing a rose in honor of their fathers. Mrs. Dodd continued to support the idea of Father's Day throughout her lifetime and is widely recognized for her role in the adoption of the holiday.

A bill to give national recognition to the holiday was introduced in Congress in 1913. Then, in 1916, President Woodrow Wilson personally observed the holiday when he spoke at a Father's Day celebration in Spokane about wanting to make the holiday official. Again, Congress resisted any attempt fearing that it would become commercialized.

President Calvin Coolidge made another attempt, in 1924, when he recommended to the individual states they hold their own observances. He did not try, however, to make any national proclamation since the two earlier attempts had already been defeated by Congress. Then, in 1926, a National Father's Day Committee was founded in New York City. Heavily supported through the years by the purveyors of male gifts, in 1966, President Lyndon Johnson finally issued the first proclamation declaring the third Sunday in June a national holiday. Finally, in 1972, President Richard Nixon made it a permanent holiday and adopted it into law.

Just as the carnation has become the symbol for Mother's Day, the rose, called for years ago by Sonora Smart Dodd, has become the flower worn by women on Father's Day. A red rose signifies that a woman's father is still living while a white rose indicates that he has passed on.

Fireworks Displays

Fireworks have been associated with celebrations in Europe for a very long time. And while they came to the United States from Europe, their origins before that are a little sketchy. The Chinese are credited with the invention of fireworks but it is possible they may have come from India. The first fireworks were so loud that the Chinese believed they would scare away evil spirits. Eventually, almost any event was considered appropriate for fireworks (i.e. births, deaths, weddings). Fireworks first began appearing in Europe in the 13th century. Traditionally, people believed that fireworks were brought to Europe from the East by Marco Polo; the Crusades are the most likely explanation. By the 15th century, they were being used widely throughout Europe for religious festivals and public entertainment.

Once called illuminations, fireworks were brought to the colonies by the first settlers. Firing black powder was used for holiday celebrations and to impress the natives. This was very popular but soon got out of control. Eventually, pranksters in Rhode Island caused enough problems that in 1731, a ban was passed on the use of fireworks for mischievous behavior. Still, fireworks continued growing in popularity for public celebrations.

On July 2, 1776, the Continental Congress voted to declare independence from England. This was celebrated with fireworks. Previously in England, fireworks had been used to celebrate the birthday of King George III, but now the colonists were using them to celebrate his mock funeral symbolizing the end of the monarchy's hold on America.

Though the Revolutionary War was still in progress, the first Independence Day was celebrated July 4, 1777 in Philadelphia, one year from signing the Declaration of Independence and the celebration included fireworks in recognition of the canons and small arms used in the war. In 1789, George Washington's inauguration included fireworks. Through the following years, fireworks became more and more associated with public celebration as Independence Day continued to be celebrated every year.

In the late 18th century, politicians began using them to attract crowds to hear their speeches. This was quite effective as the early fireworks were very loud and were enjoyed simply for their sound. It wasn't until the 1830's that color was introduced. The Italians created color by adding trace amounts of metals that burned at high temperatures. Thus, the modern firework was born.

Oktoberfest

Get out the Lederhosen and Steins! It's time for Gemütlichkeit - the festive spirit of Oktoberfest. This Bavarian festival originated in Munich, but has become so popular it is celebrated in countless cities around the world.

Oktoberfest, 16 days of drinking, eating, singing and dancing, originally began in October. Because of the bad weather at this time of the year, the festival schedule was changed in 1880. Now Oktoberfest begins on a Samstag (Saturday) in September and ends the first Sonntag (Sunday) in Oktober. With the exception of wartime, Oktoberfests have been held in Munich for almost 200 years. On opening day, the festival comes alive just as the clock of St. Paul's Church strikes twelve noon. The Burgermeister enters one of the beer tents, taps the first cask, and heartily drinks the first Stein during a 12 cannon salute.

The first Oktoberfest occurred October 17, 1810 when King Maximillian of Bavaria gave a reception to celebrate the wedding of his son, Prince Ludwig, and Princess Therese of Sachsen-Hildburghausen. Held in a large meadow (Wiese) in Munich, the entertainment included a horse race staged for 40,000 people from all over Bavaria. The party was so successful that King Maximillian decided to hold one every year in the meadow, which was then

?? WHY DO WE DO THAT ??

named Theresien-wiese after Ludwig's bride. Eventually, the horse races were replaced by agricultural shows and parades.

Oktoberfest is not just a festival…it's also a style of beer (Bier). As it happened, the 1810 wedding festival occurred just about the time the spring's stockpile of Bier had to be depleted to make room for the fall production. March (März) was the last month that Bier was made since Bier made in the warmer months usually acquired a foul taste. Being that alcohol is a natural preservative, this Bier was made with a higher alcohol content (about 5%) to get through the warmer months. Full-bodied, they are known as Oktoberfest or Marzen, contain almost no hops and have a sweet, malty taste. An Oktoberfest is brewed much like the reddish-amber Marzen that was served at Ludwig's wedding in 1810. Before refrigeration brought about a revolution in brewing, Bier was brewed in March, lagered or cold-stored in caves for 10-12 weeks, and ready to drink by the late summer or early fall.

The Oktoberfest celebration is steeped with tradition. In the Biergarten, if a stein is in one hand, the other usually holds a Wurst or sausage. The keg is tapped while the oom-pah band plays Trinklieder (drinking songs). Polka, yodeling, and a Maypole dance (Webentanz) can be seen around the Fruchtsäule (a harvest monument constructed of seeds from fresh fruits, nuts, and vegetables). Schuhplattler, a dance from the alpine country, is also performed wearing the traditional Bavarian costumes, Dirndls and Lederhosen.

As German immigrants came to the United States, smaller Oktoberfests were held in their communities and today, Munich and Cincinnati compete to be the site of the world's largest Oktoberfest.

Whether you are planning a trip to Munich or just looking for a local celebration, you should take the time to experience the warm friendliness, or Gemütlichkeit, of Oktoberfest. As they say, all work and no play…

?? WHY DO WE DO THAT ??

Giving Thanks

We've all learned about the first Thanksgiving at school where the colonists at Plymouth celebrated surviving their first year in the new world by feasting for three days with the Wampanoag Indians who helped them and taught them. Unfortunately, we were taught wrong. This wasn't the first Thanksgiving for the Pilgrims nor was it even the first Thanksgiving in America. The truth is, the colonists were Puritans and fasting and prayer during hard times followed by feasting and thanksgiving when times were good was a common practice at the time. They would have done this routinely before coming to the United States and, since others had arrived in this country long before the Mayflower, they would not have been the first to do it here. It was simply a common thing to do at that time.

Now, at this famous feast in 1621, the colonists would have been giving thanks for surviving that first hard year in the New World. Their feast did not resemble anything like we eat today. Historical records indicate that the colonists provided fowl (probably duck and geese) and the Wampanoag brought five deer. Since there would have been no ovens, sugar, flour, etc., there would have been no pies or other desserts. All the foods served would have been prepared using Wampanoag spices and methods. The games played at this gathering would have included archery and fishing and such, so how did this celebration evolve into the traditions we observe today?

As we've said, days of fasting and thanksgiving feasts were common practice back then so, in 1623, the colonists held another feast to mark the end of a long drought which had prompted Governor Bradford to call for a period of fasting. During the Revolutionary War, the Continental Congress designated one or two days of thanksgiving per year.

The first official Thanksgiving Day in the United States occurred on November 26, 1789 when George Washington issued a Thanksgiving Proclamation by the U.S. government declaring a day to be thankful for the Constitution of the United States. On this day money was also sent to debtors in prison becoming the first known instance of charity on Thanksgiving. Expressions and feelings of thanks just naturally lead to charity and this continues to be a tradition today. This Thanksgiving Day proclamation was opposed by Thomas Jefferson on the grounds of separation of church and state. Similar proclamations were made by the presidents which followed, John Adams (also opposed by Tom Jefferson) and James Madison.

In 1817, New York became the first state to make Thanksgiving a state holiday and many others followed suit. The states of the Deep South, however, did not embrace the holiday. In 1827, author and editor of the popular women's magazine

"Godey's Lady's Book", Sarah Josepha Hale, launched a lengthy campaign to make Thanksgiving a national holiday. This took a long time, but eventually, in 1863, Abraham Lincoln declared Thanksgiving a national holiday. He was hoping it would help the country to focus on things which they could be thankful for rather than focusing on the Civil War.

The Thanksgiving Day holiday was set as the last Thursday in November and was celebrated as such until, in 1939, Franklin Roosevelt moved it back one week in response to retailers' concerns that the Christmas selling season was made too short by it. He believed that the change would help spur the economy during the Great Depression. This caused a great public outcry and people began referring to the holiday as 'Franksgiving'. Finally, in 1941, he reluctantly signed a bill changing the holiday to the 4th Thursday of the month.

Every Thanksgiving since Lincoln declared it a holiday in 1863, the President of the United States has issued a Thanksgiving Day Proclamation. In this speech, the President offers his ideas about what he thinks the holiday stands for thus giving us an insight into what he believes we, as a country, have to be thankful for. And, beginning in 1947, each year the President pardons a turkey from slaughter and it is sent to a retirement farm to live its life free from the threat of the dining room table.

But how did the turkey become the bird of choice?? It's unlikely that turkey was served way back when at Plymouth. Some say it's due to Benjamin Franklin, at one time, campaigning to make the turkey the national bird. Some say it has to do with a Norman Rockwell painting of a family gathering around a turkey dinner. The other foods we eat at Thanksgiving are not exactly the wild roots and corn the Pilgrims and Wampanoag would have eaten either and vary by your location and culture. I guess it's a mystery.

Thanksgiving Day parades were held in various places in the states before Thanksgiving became a national holiday. The first big Thanksgiving Day parade was held in Philadelphia in 1920 by Gimbels. The parade ended with Santa arriving at Gimbels Department Store on Market Street, climbing up a fire ladder, and entering the toy department through a window. In 1924, Macy's began holding their parade when a group of employees wanted to celebrate the holiday similar to how they had in Europe. The annual parades began, quite simply, as marketing tools by retailers to launch the Christmas selling season.

The first Thanksgiving football game occurred in 1876 between Yale and Princeton. Since that time, many teams have chosen to play on this day. The Dallas Cowboys and the Detroit Lions regularly hold games on Thanksgiving. Simply, it is a day when spectators are off work and can attend.

As you can see, though we've been taught the origins of Thanksgiving began in Plymouth, none of our traditions actually started there or resemble what was done there. Our Thanksgiving feast simply evolved from a common practice of the time which was, of course, also the reason the Pilgrims observed the feast. While the two have common origins, one apparently did not originate from the other.

Hanukkah (or Chanukah)

Hanukkah is an eight day holiday which marks the miraculous victory of the Jews, led by the Maccabees, against Greek persecution and religious oppression. In addition to being victorious in war, a miracle occurred. When they came to rededicate the Temple, they found only one flask of oil with which to light the Menorah. This small flask lasted for eight days. In order to commemorate this miracle, Jews light a Menorah for the eight days of Hanukkah.

Hanukkah is not a Jewish version of Christmas. Although it is celebrated the same time of year, Hanukkah commemorates the physical and spiritual victory of the Jews over the Greeks more than 2,000 years ago.

Hanukkah is also known as the:
Festival of Lights, since the flame in the Temple burned miraculously for eight days.
Feast of Dedication, since the Temple was rededicated after being desecrated.

Hanukkah is celebrated from 25 Kislev - 2 Tevet, according to the Jewish calendar, which is lunar, so it falls on different dates each year. Remember that all Jewish holidays begin at sundown the evening before.

One way Hanukkah is celebrated is through food.

?? WHY DO WE DO THAT ??

Because the oil in the lamps lasted for eight days, during Hanukkah Jewish people eat foods fried in oil. Most often this is latkes (fried potato pancakes) and deep fried donuts. Cheese is also eaten in remembrance of how one of the greatest victories against the Maccabees was gained by feeding the enemy cheese.

Children play with the dreidel in remembrance of the brave children who lived during the time of the conquering Greeks. Every effort was made by the Greeks to force Hellenism upon the Jews at the expense of teaching Jewish Law and the Torah schools were closed. Hence, Jewish Law had to be taught to the children in secret in the forest. When the Greek patrols would come by, the children would hide their books and play with tops to cover what they were doing in the woods. Today, four Hebrew letters are on the dreidel and they are an acronym for "Nes Gadol Hayah Sham"—a great miracle happened there.

Because Hanukkah is associated so closely with the education of children, it is also customary to give Chanukah gelt (money) to children on each of the 8 days of the season. This enables the children to be taught about giving to charity from out of what one has in order to honor G-d. The Jews remember that the Greeks did not take their possessions but rather defiled them by using them for impure pursuits.

Spiritually, Jews celebrate Hanukkah in the morning

prayer service each day by reciting the complete Hallel (Psalms 113-118) and reading from the Torah about the offerings brought at the dedication of the Tabernacle. This is a reminder to them of the Maccabean rededication of the Temple after it had been defiled by the Greeks. A special prayer of thanksgiving (V'al Hanissim) is also inserted in the prayers and grace after meals during Hanukkah.

It is intended that the Menorah be lit by every Jew everywhere during Hanukkah in remembrance of the Menorah that burned miraculously for eight days. Candles can be used but ideally, olive oil is considered to be more representative. In the Torah, we see the Menorah in the first and second Temples described as having had seven branches. After the Temples' destruction, a tradition arose among the Jewish people that nothing from the Temple should be duplicated so Menorahs began to appear having six branches. The Hanukkah Menorah, however, has nine branches: eight to hold the oil or candles to be burned during the eight days of Hanukkah and one to hold the Shamash, which is used to light the other candles.

First Fruits of the Harvest

The 1960s were a time of racial tension in this country and much was heard about civil rights, black power, and the Black Freedom Movement. It was a volatile time. And right in the midst of all this, on August 11, 1965, a riot broke out in Watts, a minority area of Los Angeles, CA. It seems that the police had arrested a motorist named Marquette Frye and people believed that the police had treated him too roughly. Now, the people of that area had already been angry for a while about racism, poverty, and poor housing conditions and this incident set off a riot that went on for four days. Police and passing cars were bombarded by flying bricks, pieces of concrete, etc. and the havoc was unbelievable. Four thousand people were arrested, hundreds were injured, and 34 were killed. Afterwards, Watts looked like a war zone with extensive destruction and looting, many people were left homeless, and businesses moved away. However, something had changed. People began joining together to rebuild and help try and make the community stronger.

A young man named Maulana Karenga was in his last year of graduate school at the time of the riots. It was his belief that the people had lost touch with their African heritage. He wanted to restore a sense of unity among the people and a pride in their culture. Karenga began researching ancient African harvest celebrations to learn more about them.

These harvest first fruit celebrations were celebrated throughout Africa by various tribes and dated back as far as the ancient civilizations of Nubia and Egypt. Though practiced differently by the diverse tribes on the continent, the ideas of unity and community seemed to be universal. These celebrations were a way of giving thanks and rewarding tribal members for their teamwork during the year.

The Kwanzaa holiday was created in 1966 by Maulana Karenga and designed to incorporate these African cultural roots, thus tying African-Americans to each other through their native Motherland. The holiday's name comes from the Swahili term "matunda ya kwanza" which means "first fruits of the harvest". Swahili was chosen since it is the most commonly used language in Africa and many of the words and phrases used in the Kwanzaa observance are Swahili.

Originally, Karenga intended Kwanzaa to replace the celebration of Christmas so that African-Americans would have their own holiday rather than observing that of the dominant culture. However, he later changed that position to allow practicing Christians to be able to participate since Kwanzaa is, by definition, not a religious holiday but rather a celebration of family, community, and culture. Hence, today, some African-Americans celebrate only Kwanzaa while others celebrate both Kwanzaa and Christmas. The dates December 26th through January 1st were chosen for the observance. This avoids the commercial buying season of the holidays but stills falls at the time of heightened holiday spirit.

Kwanzaa is based on the Nguzo Saba, which in Swahili means "seven guiding principles". Each of the seven days of Kwanzaa focuses on one of the seven principles:

- UMOJA (unity) – to strive for and maintain unity in the family, community, nation, and race
- KUJICHAGULIA (self-determination) – to define ourselves, name ourselves, create for ourselves and speak for ourselves
- UJIMA (collective work and responsibility) – to build and maintain our community together and make our brother's and sister's problems our problems and to solve them together
- UJAMAA (cooperative economics) – to build and maintain our own stores, shops, and other businesses and to profit from them together
- NIA (purpose) – to make our collective vocation the building and developing of our community in order to restore our people to their traditional greatness
- KUUMBA (creativity) – to do always as much as we can, in the way we can, in order to leave our community more beautiful and beneficial than we inherited it

- IMANI (faith) – to believe with all our heart in our people, our parents, our teachers, our leaders, and the righteousness and victory of our struggle

During Kwanzaa, a family displays two important items: a poster of the guiding principles and a bendera. Bendera is Swahili for flag and the Kwanzaa flag is made up of the three Kwanzaa colors:

- Black – represents the people and comes from their color
- Red – represents the blood shed in their struggle
- Green – represents the future hope that comes through struggle and comes from the fertile grounds of the motherland

There are seven basic symbols used in the celebration of Kwanzaa which are prominently displayed in the home:

- MAZAO (crops) – symbolizes the harvest or the rewards of collective labor
- MKEKA (mat) – symbolizes tradition and history (made of straw; other symbols are placed on this mat)
- KINARA (candle holder) – symbolizes roots in the people of the motherland
- MUHINDI (corn) – symbolizes children and the future they embody (one ear for each child in the family; if there are no children,

two ears are placed to represent the village's responsibility to help raise the children)
- MISHUMAA (seven candles) – symbolize the Seven Principles (one black, three red, three green)
- KIKOMBE cha UMOJA (unity cup) – symbolizes practice of unity (contains the libation to be used during the evening ceremonies)
- ZAWADI (gifts) – symbolize labor and love of parents and the commitments made and kept by the children (usually handmade and/or African items; given on the last day mostly to children but must include a book and a heritage symbol)

4 MISCELLANEOUS TRADITIONS

Birthday Parties, Hats, and Cards

Many years ago in Europe, people believed that evil spirits would seek out a person on their birthday and haunt them. Not just ordinary people, but especially the king. For this reason, people would gather together to protect that person on his or her birthday and bring them good wishes. This was accomplished by surrounding them and making merry. It was important to make a lot of noise in order to scare away the evil spirits.

These early birthday parties were only for the wealthy. This was partly due to the fact that the evil spirits sought out mostly the king but also because only the very rich could afford to throw these lavish parties. Additionally, commoners in those times were not well educated and were not able to read calendars and know when people's birthdays occurred. For this reason, the birthday crown became a popular party favor and led to the current tradition of wearing party hats. Eventually, those unable to come and bring their good wishes in person started sending cards (this started in England approximately 100 years ago).

Birthday Cakes

I think we can all agree that a birthday party just wouldn't be the same without a cake, right? But these wonderful creations haven't always been served at parties. Where did the first birthday cakes come from?

It seems the early Greeks first used round or moon shaped cakes and took them to the Temple of their Goddess Artemis. These cakes were shaped to represent the moon and were more like bread than the cakes we eat today. They were sweetened with honey and called plakons which is similar to the word for flat. Candles were lit on the cake to make it glow like the moon. It was believed that the smoke from the candles would carry their prayers to the gods.

Credit for candles on cakes is also given to the Germans who began in the Middle Ages a practice of baking sweetened bread dough shaped like baby Jesus in memory of His birthday. These were seen again later at celebrations known as Kinderfest, a German child's celebration of their birthday and became a Geburtstagorten, a sweeter birthday version baked in layers. A large candle was placed in the center of the cake to represent the 'light of life'. It wasn't until the 'Happy Birthday' song became popular in the early 1900's that the words 'Happy Birthday' began to be printed on the cakes.

Birthday cakes were originally a privilege enjoyed only by the wealthy due to cost but with the Industrial Revolution, the ingredients and tools required for baking these treats made them accessible to the common man and they began to be enjoyed by more and more people. And with the advent of the 'Happy Birthday' song, people began to blow out their candles after making a birthday wish.

On a particularly unappetizing note: The word cake is derived from the Norse word 'kaka'.

Baby Showers

The arrival of infants is celebrated in almost every culture. In the United States, the modern baby shower is a fun way to welcome a new little one into the world. And since it is practiced almost exclusively in the United States, most people would be surprised to learn that this custom has its origins from outside sources.

In Ancient Egypt and Rome, homemade gifts of clothing, food, and blankets were often given to new parents after the birth of a child. This was usually something of a higher monetary value to help the family get started but also served as an opportunity for the gift-givers to come and see the new arrival. It is believed by some that the arrival of the Magi at Christ's birth was an influencer of this practice.

During the Middle Ages, it became customary for godparents to present babies with gifts at their christening... often a pair of silver spoons. It became quite the temptation for parents to appoint more and more godparents for their children. Eventually, the church found it necessary to put a limit on the number of godparents each baby could have.

Hundreds of years ago, people would bring new mothers gifts of useful items. They would wait until the baby was at least one month of age, because it was believed that newborn infants were susceptible to illness. Then, when it was safe, the baby would be introduced to friends and family at a major event... a Christening perhaps.

During the Victorian Era, woman began to hold tea parties for the mother. At that time, it was customary to attend such events carrying a parasol and so the practice of placing the gifts inside the parasol began and the umbrella is still used today as the symbol of a shower.

As years went by, women began celebrating before the baby was born and it was the 20th century that saw the baby shower change to its current form. At the end of WWII, during the baby boom, it became common for friends and family (women only) to gather at a party and celebrate a new baby. These parties were usually only held for first babies and were intended to pass on the wisdom and knowledge the new mother needed. Baby showers have continued ever since and today it is common for even dads and siblings to join in the fun.

Bridal Showers

Wherever there's a bride and a wedding, you can pretty much count on at least one bridal shower prior to the big event. These have become an American mainstay allowing a young woman's friends and family to help her celebrate her joy and prepare for her coming marriage. And while the bridal shower, as we know it, is relatively new in this country, its origins go back quite a way to the days when dowries had to be provided by the bride's family to help the groom with the expenses of establishing a new household.

In the 1300s, there was a British custom known as Bruydale, or bride ale. The day before the wedding a party would be held. The bride would sell her very own homemade beer at high prices to her guests to boost her dowry.

However, tradition has it that the bridal shower really got started in Holland in the 1500s-1600s. As the story goes, a young Dutch girl who was the daughter of a prominent business man in town fell in love with a local miller. Now it's said that this miller was very generous, often giving away free bread to those who couldn't pay, so that he was much richer in friends than he was in coins. The girl's father, wanting her to marry better, forbid her to ever see the miller, refusing to pay her dowry. The townsfolk, being extremely fond of the miller, devised a plan where each would bring a small gift to the young couple and collectively provide all that was needed to establish a new household. Upon hearing of this, the father was so moved, that he changed his mind and blessed the union. This was considered so successful that people continued showering couples with gifts after that.

In the Victorian era, upper middle class ladies spent most of their lives prior to marriage filling their hope chests and usually had what they needed when they were ready to marry. However, for camaraderie (and something to do), they would often hold bridal showers to celebrate the excitement of an upcoming wedding. These parties usually involved holding a parasol filled with gifts over the bride-to-be and opening it over her head thus showering her with useful presents. (I suspect there were no toasters at these early parties.)

The traditional shower, as we know it today, started around the 1920s. Friends and family would drop by the bride's home spontaneously and bring gifts. By the 1930s, the practice had spread to rural areas, as well. While bridal showers are not usually a surprise to the bride any more, they are still a very popular tradition.

Mazel Tov

As in all things Hebrew, the Jewish practice of breaking a glass at the conclusion of a wedding is steeped in meaning. There are many explanations offered for this tradition and what it represents, as it dates back to one of the world's most ancient civilizations, but the most commonly offered is that it is a reminder of the destruction of the Temple in Jerusalem. The use of a wine glass, and wine, in the wedding ceremony, is all part of linking the wedding ritual with Jewish history and the people's relationship with G_d.

The glass to be used in the wedding can be any glass but most choose a special one to be kept afterwards. Traditionally, a wine glass is used as wine was an important part of many Jewish rituals in the Old Testament. This was because wine was a luxury in the ancient civilization and is now used throughout the wedding ceremony to symbolize the importance of the occasion.

In the consecration of the wedding ceremony, the Rabbi gives the marriage blessing over the wine glass. Then, the bride and groom drink from this same wine glass symbolizing their union under G_d. During the actual ceremony, the Rabbi blesses the wine while praising and thanking G_d for the ability to unite the couple in marriage. This is followed by the "Sheva Berachot", the Seven Blessings, which are said over the glass of wine. Once this is done, the bride and groom drink the glass of wine. When the wedding is complete, the glass is wrapped in cloth and the groom stomps on the glass, breaking it with his right foot and the crowd shouts, "Mazel Tov!" This is Yiddish for "Good Fortune" and is equivalent to 'Congratulations' or 'Good Luck'. Breaking the glass is a symbolic way of saying the marriage is meant to be 'irrevocable and permanent'.

Jumping the Broom

For African-American people, the term "Jumping the Broom" is just as synonymous with "getting married" as the term "tying the knot". In practice, it involves a bride and a groom holding hands while standing in front of a broomstick and taking a leap into a new life together. It can occur at the wedding or at the reception, but is always after they are declared man and wife. This act is a symbol of sweeping away the old life and welcoming the new and represents the joining of two families.

Many people believe this practice originated in Ghana, a country in Africa. At weddings in Ghana, a broomstick was waved over the couple's heads to ward off evil spirits. Sometimes, but not always, at the end of the ceremony, the couple would jump over the broomstick. For the bride, this was a declaration of her willingness to clean and care for her new home. But the practice was also to determine the nature of the union. Whichever of the two jumped higher would dominate the household throughout the marriage.

There are also many people who say there is no evidence of this practice in Ghana. Since Wiccans and Gypsies also have jumping the broom traditions, they believe that the practice may be European in origin. Still others believe that the practice originated with the American slaves themselves. No one knows the truth for sure.

During the days of slavery, it was believed that if slaves were allowed to marry and form family bonds it would make them stronger. It was feared that they might organize and rebel so marriage among slaves was made illegal. Because they were not allowed legally sanctioned marriages, the slaves sought to establish a way of legitimizing the union of a couple, bonding them before God, in a way as close to marriage as possible. Jumping the broom became the vehicle for accomplishing this. As it happened, the slaves were also denied the right to practice any traditional rituals from their culture. But a few rituals were considered to be harmless and were still allowed to be practiced and jumping the broom was one of them.

After the slaves were emancipated, they were allowed to have legal marriages and the practice of jumping the broom was almost completely abandoned in favor of legitimate unions. This was understandable since jumping the broom had always been a substitute for the real thing and carried the stigma of slavery. However, in 1977, when the miniseries "Roots" was aired on television, a scene which featured the ritual brought it into the spotlight and its popularity in modern weddings has been growing rapidly. Today, the practice is a remembrance of ancestors in slavery who did not have the same freedoms their descendants now enjoy.

?? WHY DO WE DO THAT ??

Saving the Morning Light

While serving as U.S. ambassador to France in 1784, Benjamin Franklin suggested to the Parisians that by rising earlier, they could make use of the morning sunlight to accomplish more of their daily tasks thus saving on candle wax. Way back then, the Parisians were known for sleeping well past noon. Though Ben never actually suggested changing the time on the clocks, he is often credited with inventing daylight saving time as well as the phrase, "Early to bed, early to rise, makes a man healthy, wealthy and wise."

The idea to actually change the clocks was proposed in 1895 by a shift worker in New Zealand named George Vernon Hudson. Because Hudson did shift work, he had extra time in the evenings to pursue insect collecting. George Hudson proposed that the clocks be moved two hours in the summer to allow for additional sunlight time in the evenings so that he could pursue entomology. The clocks could then be returned to 'standard' time in the fall to bring the sunlight back to the morning hours. Though this was never implemented in Hudson's lifetime, he did go on to become a famous entomologist.

In 1905, a builder named William Willett began proposing the idea in England but Daylight Saving Time never became a reality until WWI. It was implemented in 1916 in Manitoba, followed shortly by Germany and its allies and then a little later by Britain and her allies. It was intended as a means to conserve coal (and incandescent lighting) during the war. Russia followed suit and implemented in 1917 with the United States finally coming around in 1918. While it is still practiced today and continues to provide extended sunlight in the summer evenings, it is quite controversial and the debate continues over whether it ever actually helped to conserve any energy. It remains the subject of much lobbying in our nation's capital.

?? WHY DO WE DO THAT ??

ABOUT THE AUTHOR

DJ Selvidge has always had an avid interest in exploring the rich cultural backgrounds that make up this great country of ours. At one time she was a regular contributor to her employer's Diversity newsletter and in this capacity, began discovering how intensely fascinating the origins of some of our most common traditions really were. She decided that she would like to someday research the origins of common traditions and this book is the result.

DJ has previously written a fictional book about what life is like in a Kansas foster home called "A Sibling Group of Three" hoping to raise public awareness of the problems involved with a state/legal system raising children.

DJ lives with her husband and family in Wichita, KS.

ALSO BY THIS AUTHOR

Marie and Edward Worthington are typical empty-nesters. They hold down normal jobs during the day and come home to a peaceful house at night... that is, until they decide they miss the kids and become foster parents for the state. After a grueling six-month process, they finally have their residential license and receive their first foster care placement, a sibling group of three. As Marie drives to the youth shelter to pick up the Kingsley children, she is optimistic. These children have led such disadvantaged and neglected lives, and she is sure they will appreciate being in a good environment. This is the story of her coming of age. It is a journey where both the characters and the reader emerge more knowledgeable about the realities of the bureaucratic foster care system and how it functions in our society.

http://www.amazon.com/Sibling-Group-Three-DJ-Selvidge-ebook/dp/B009MFHR5A/ref=sr_1_1?ie=UTF8&qid=1435093249&sr=8-1&keywords=dj+selvidge